Titles in This Series

My Alphabet Book
My Counting Book
My Book of Colors and Shapes
My Book of Opposites

LADYBIRD BOOKS, INC.
Auburn, Maine 04210 U.S.A.
© LADYBIRD BOOKS LTD MCMLXXXVIII
Loughborough, Leicestershire, England

Printed in England

My Alphabet Book

illustrated by TERRY BURTON

Ladybird Books

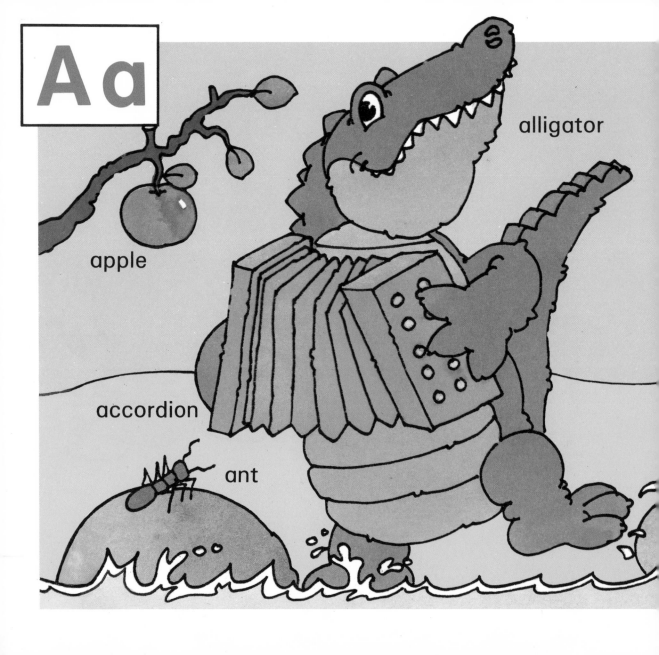

A a

apple

alligator

accordion

ant

Cc

camel

cat

candles

cake

F f

fox

fence

fin

fish

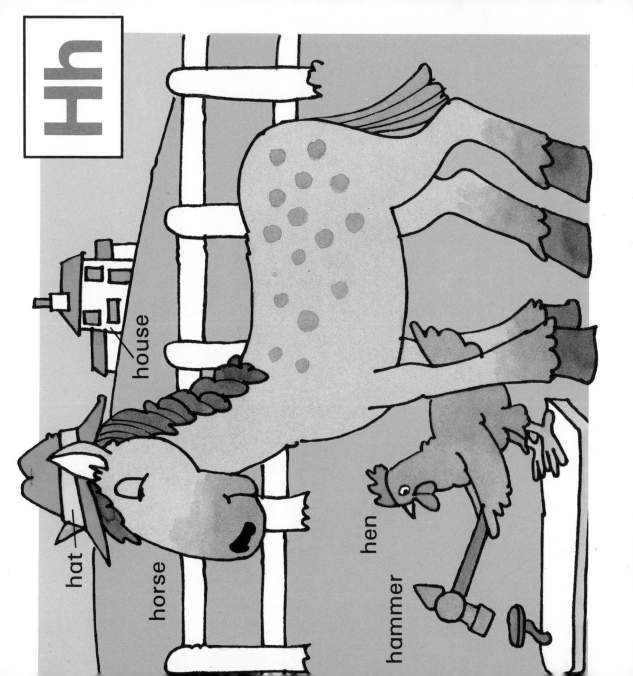

Hh

house

hat

horse

hen

hammer

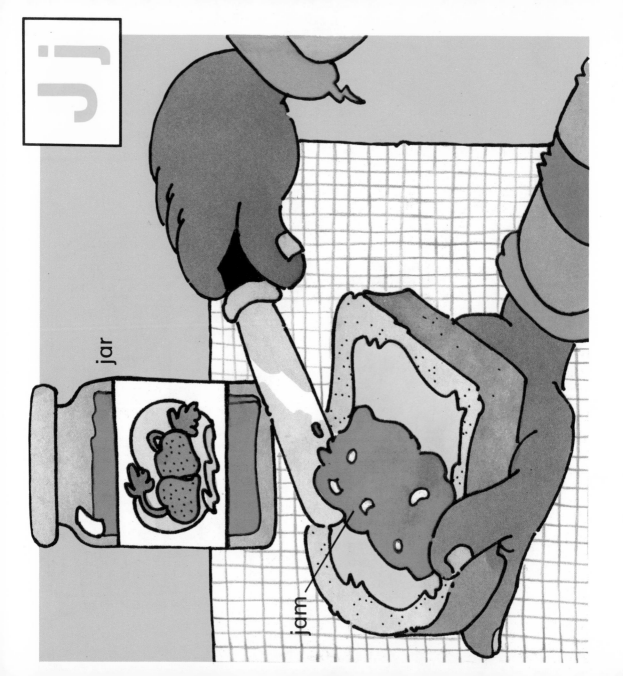

Jj

jar

jam

K k

kangaroo

kettle

king

Mm

moon

mirror

mouse

monkey

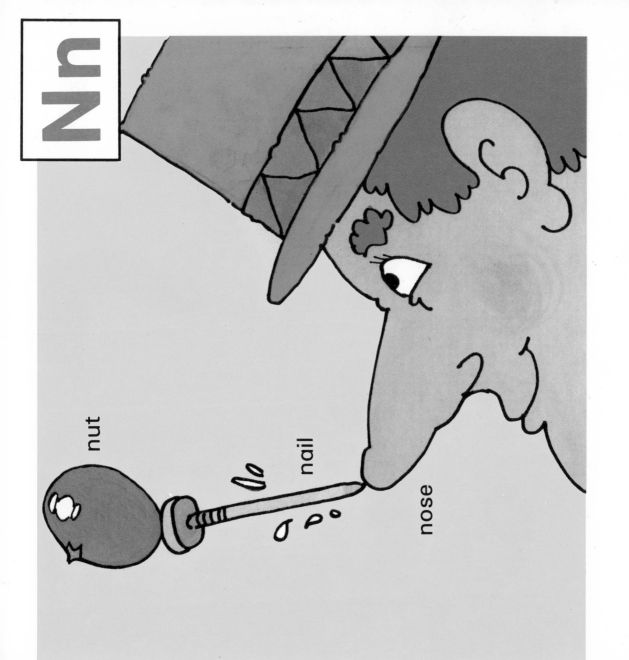

Nn

nut

nail

nose

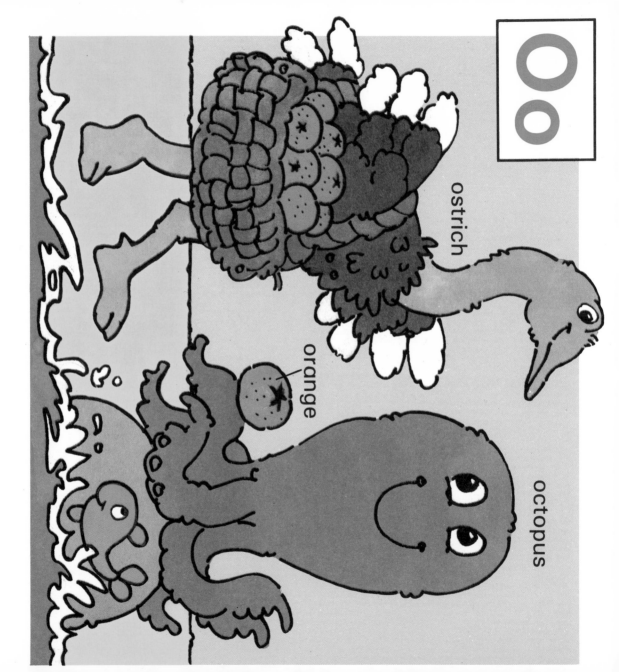

ostrich

orange

octopus

Pp

panda

pen

pencil

paper

penguin

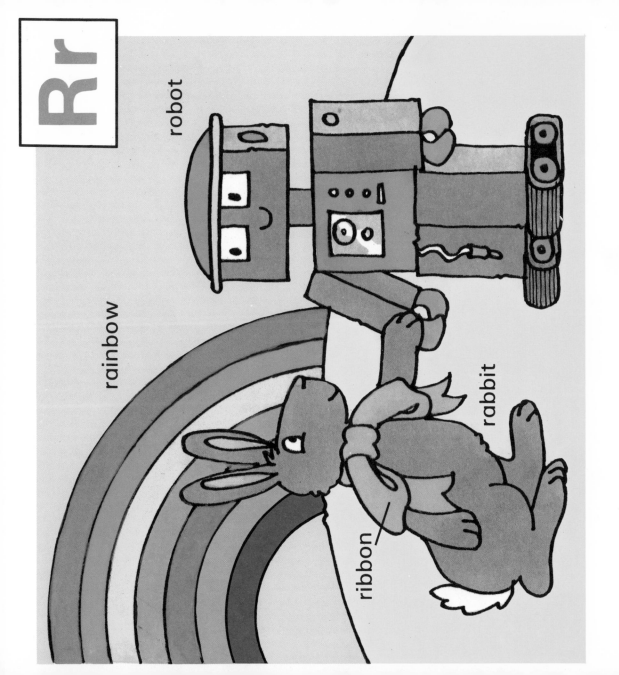

Ss

seesaw

sock

sun

Tt

tomatoes

tiger

telephone

table

Uu

umbrella

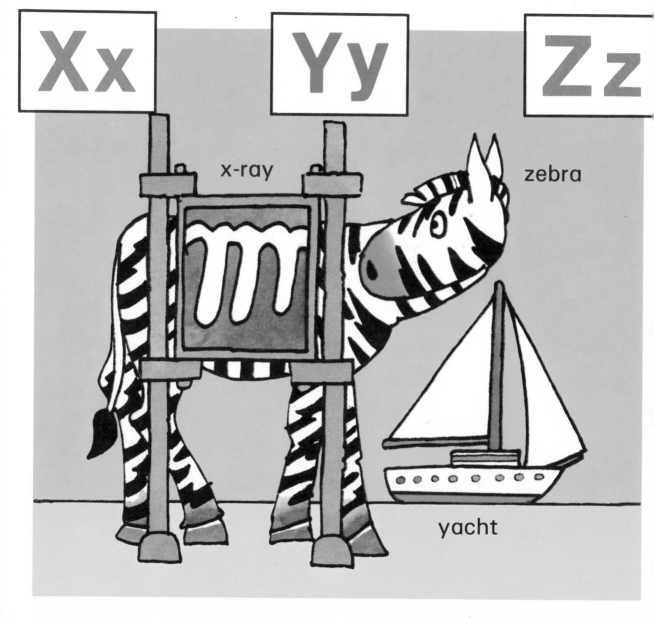

Xx

Yy

Zz

x-ray

zebra

yacht

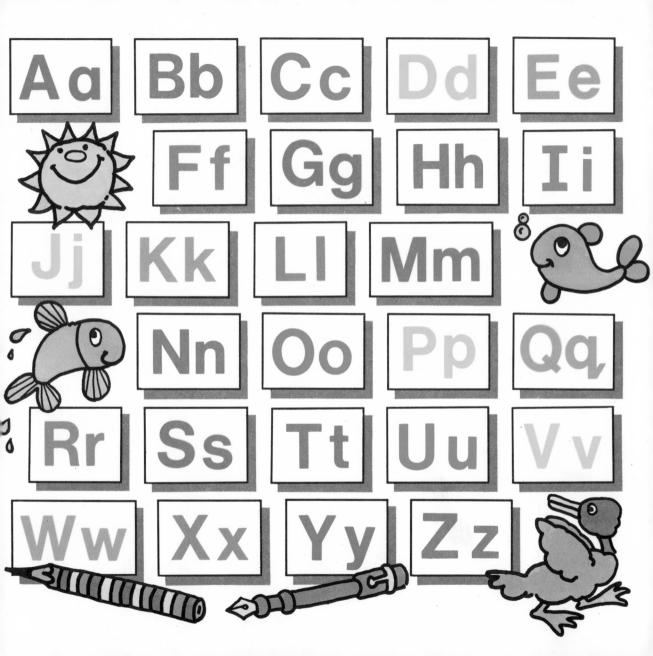